The Young Scientist Investigates

Air

by
Terry Jennings

#393

CP CHILDRENS PRESS®
CHICAGO

Woodland Presbyterian School

Illustrated by
John Barber
Karen Daws
Gary Hincks
Tony Morris
Tudor Artists

Library of Congress Cataloging-in-Publication Data

Jennings, Terry J.
    Air / by Terry Jennings.
       p. cm. — (The Young scientist investigates)
    Originally published: Oxford : Oxford University Press, 1982.
    Includes index.
    Summary: An introduction to the composition of air and its
importance to each and every living thing. Includes study
questions, activities, and experiments.
    ISBN 0-516-08435-6
    1. Air—Juvenile literature. [1. Air.] I. Title. II. Series:
Jennings, Terry J. Young scientist investigates.
QC161.2.J46   1989
533'.6—dc 19   89-453
                                                CIP
                                              AC

North American edition published in 1989 by
Childrens Press®, Inc.

© Terry Jennings 1982
First published 1982 by Oxford University Press

Printed in the United States of America
1 2 3 4 5 6 7 8 9 10 R 98 97 96 95 94 93 92 91 90 89

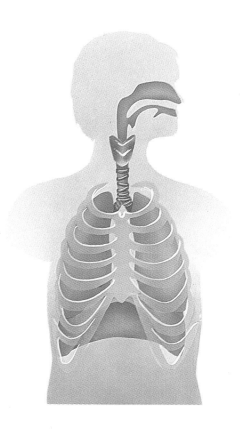

The Young Scientist Investigates
Air

Contents

Air is everywhere

Air is all around us. Although we look through air all the time, we never see it. Nor can we smell air or taste it. Yet air is everywhere. How can we tell that air is there when we cannot see it? We can feel the air when it blows on our face. We can hear the air on a windy day as it rushes along.

We live at the bottom of a big layer of air. This layer of air around the earth is called the atmosphere. At ground level, there is plenty of air. As we go higher and higher, there is less and less air. Hundreds of miles up in the sky there is no air at all. Then we are in space. There is no air in space.

Atmosphere

There is less air on high mountains than at ground level.

2

Air and our bodies

Everyone must breathe air to live. Air has several gases in it. The most important of these gases is oxygen. When we breathe in, air enters through our nose. The air goes down a tube called the windpipe into our lungs. Our lungs are like two large, spongy bags in our chest. We can feel our chest getting bigger as we breathe in. Inside our lungs, some of the oxygen from the air goes into our blood. The blood takes the oxygen to every part of our body.

When we breathe out, there is more of a gas called carbon dioxide in the air that comes out of our mouth. The air that comes out is also wetter. You can see the little drops of water if you breathe onto a cold mirror.

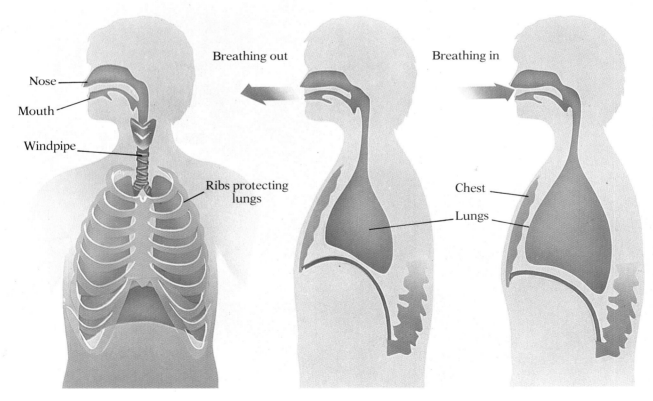

Nose

Mouth

Windpipe

Ribs protecting
lungs

Breathing out

Breathing in

Chest

Lungs

Oxygen

Diver

A crowded room often feels stuffy if the windows are not open. There is not much oxygen because the people in the room have used it up. In a stuffy room we feel tired and sleepy and have little energy. If the windows are opened, we soon feel better again.

Some people work in places where there is not much air. There is not much air near the tops of very high mountains. So mountain climbers often take their own oxygen with them. Divers working underwater also need air to breathe. Some divers carry air in tanks on their backs. Other divers, who go deep down in the water, get air from a tube. The tube goes to a pump in a boat.

Fire fighters wearing breathing equipment

Astronaut. The tubes carry oxygen to him.

In space there is no air at all. So astronauts take oxygen with them. Fire fighters sometimes have to wear tanks of air when they are putting out a very smoky fire. There may be so much smoke that there is little air for the fire fighters to breathe. Sometimes when people are very ill, the doctor gives them oxygen to breathe.

How other living things breathe

No animal, large or small, can live without air. Most of the bigger animals that live on land take in air through their lungs as we do. Some small animals have other ways of breathing. Insects have tiny holes along their sides. Air goes into the insects' bodies through these little holes. Earthworms take in oxygen straight through their thin skin. Slugs and snails breathe through quite a large hole in their sides. You can see the breathing hole on the slug in the picture.

Water beetles cannot stay underwater all the time. A water beetle comes to the surface and sticks the tip of its tail out into the air. It picks up a bubble of air and takes it underwater. The beetle breathes the air in the bubble through little tubes in its tail end. Fishes get their oxygen from air that is dissolved in water. A fish uses its gills to take oxygen out of the water. You can see this air when water is heated in a saucepan. The air comes out of the water in bubbles.

Breathing holes in the side of an insect's body

Breathing hole of slug

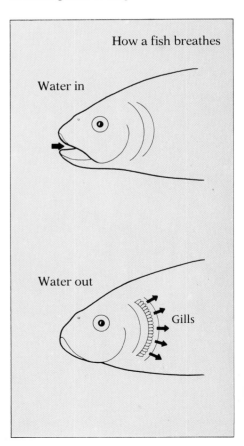

How a fish breathes

Water in

Water out

Gills

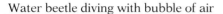

Water beetle diving with bubble of air

6

Plants and the air

Like all living things, plants breathe. They take in air through pores (tiny holes) in their leaves. But plants can do something else with air. They can make food with it in their leaves.

Sunshine

Oxygen

Carbon dioxide

Pores on the underside of a plant leaf as seen through a microscope

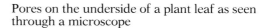
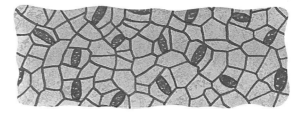

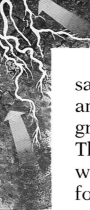

Water and mineral salts

Trees planted in a town

To make food, leaves need water and mineral salts from the soil. Leaves also need sunshine and a gas, carbon dioxide, from the air. The green substance in leaves is called chlorophyll. This green chlorophyll uses sunshine to turn water, mineral salts and carbon dioxide into food for the plant.

Oxygen is one of the waste materials plants release when they make their food. The oxygen goes into the air. Green plants are very important to all living things. They provide food for humans and other animals. In sunlight, plants make the oxygen that all living things need. Without green plants the oxygen in the air would be used up. That is why it is important, particularly in towns, to have plenty of trees and other plants.

7

Wind

When it is windy you can feel the air. Wind is moving air. The air moves because it has been warmed by the sun. If you hold your hand just above a hot radiator, you can feel hot air rising. The radiator heats the air and the hot air rises. The hot air rises because it is lighter than the cold air around it. Cooler air moves in to take the warm air's place.

The same thing happens when the sun warms the land. The land warms the air and the warm air rises. Cold air moves in to take its place. This is happening all the time somewhere in the world. We call these movements of the air, wind. Light winds are called breezes. Stronger winds are called storms and gales.

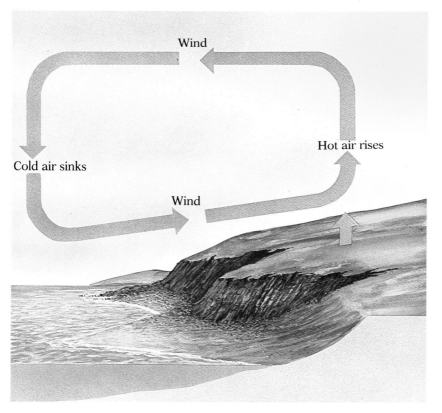

Wind

Cold air sinks

Hot air rises

Wind

Stormy weather

Storm clouds seen from space

8

Modern windmills used to make electricity

Moving air is very powerful. People can use this power in several ways. Sails are fitted to yachts to make the wind push them along. Moving air was once used a lot to drive windmills. The windmills crushed wheat to make flour. Even today some windmills are used to pump water from the ground or to make electricity.

A windmill once used to crush wheat

How a windmill works

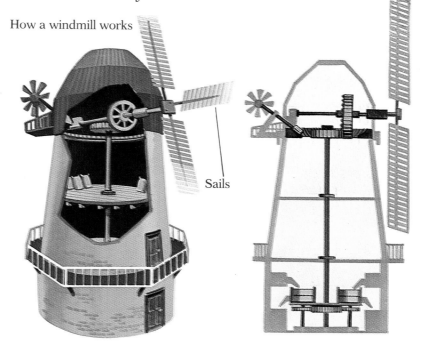

Sails

Compressed air

When you blow up a balloon you are squeezing a lot of air into a small space. When you let go of the balloon, the air rushes out again. Air can be squeezed a lot. You could squeeze all the air in a room into a few small balloons. Air that has been squeezed a lot is called compressed air. A bicycle pump squeezes or compresses air.

We can make compressed air do work for us. We use it in bicycle and car tires. Tires filled with compressed air are soft to ride on so that we do not feel the bumps in the road. Compressed air drives the drills that workers use to dig up the road. Compressed air is also used to fire the torpedoes from a submarine.

How is compressed air being used in this picture?

Blowing up a balloon

Pumping up a car tire

This drill is powered by compressed air.

Air pressure

We can pump the air out of something until it is empty. Then there is a vacuum inside. A vacuum is a completely empty space.

When something has a vacuum inside, the air outside presses hard against it. If you suck the air out of a thin plastic bottle, the bottle will go flat because the air outside is pressing on it. Air presses because, although it is very light, it does weigh something. Air is so light that it takes about 800 bottles of air to weigh as much as one bottle of water. But because air is piled hundreds of miles above the earth, it pushes downwards.

We are so used to air pressing on us that we do not notice it. The air pressure changes from day to day. These changes in the air pressure affect the weather we have. We measure these changes in air pressure with a barometer.

A plastic bottle from which the air has been sucked

A barometer

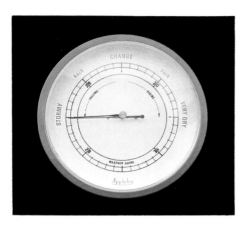

A television weather forecaster. What does the word LOW in the picture mean?

Do you remember?

(Look for the answers in the part of the book you have just been reading if you do not know them.)

1 How do we know that there is air all around us?

2 What is the big layer of air called that covers the earth?

3 What happens to your chest when you breathe in?

4 What are our lungs like?

5 What happens to the oxygen we breathe in?

6 How is the air we breathe out different from the air we breathe in?

7 Why does a crowded room feel stuffy?

8 How do divers working underwater get the air they need to breathe?

9 How do insects breathe?

10 Where do fishes get their oxygen from?

11 How do plants breathe?

12 What is the green substance in plant leaves called?

13 Why are green plants important to all living things?

14 What happens to air when it is warmed?

15 How can we use the power of moving air or wind?

16 What do we call air that has been squeezed a lot?

17 What is a vacuum?

18 Why does air press downwards?

19 Why do we not notice the air pressing down on us?

20 How do we measure changes in the air pressure?

Things to do

1 **Pouring air.** Sink a small glass in a bowl of water so that it fills with water. Stand it mouth downward on the bottom. Now push another glass rim first to the bottom of the bowl without allowing water to seep in. Air is now trapped in the second glass. Now push the glasses together and gently tilt them. Can you pour air from the second glass into the first?

2   An experiment with tissues. Cram some paper tissues tightly into the bottom of a jam jar. Be sure the tissues do not fall out. Fill a deep bowl with water. Turn the jar upside down and push it straight to the bottom of the bowl so that it is completely covered with water. Do not let go of the jar. Lift it out of the water. What has happened to the tissues? Why is this?

3   Pretend that you wish to climb Mount Everest. Mount Everest is the highest mountain in the world. It is 29,000 feet high. You will need to take tanks of oxygen with you, since there will be very little air near the top of the mountain. Write a story about your climb and the adventures you meet with.

4   How heavy is air? Find an old ruler that is no longer of any use, or a piece of thin wood that is about the same size as a ruler.

Place the ruler on the edge of a table so that the middle of the ruler is just at the table's edge. With the side of your hand, sharply strike the part of the ruler that juts out. What happens?

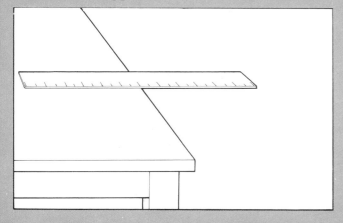

Now put the ruler on the table again in the same position as before. Carefully cover the piece of the ruler that is on the tabletop with a sheet of newspaper. Again strike the part of the ruler that juts out sharply with the side of your hand. What happens? Why is there a difference? Is it the weight of the paper that has made the difference?

5   An experiment with a bottle. Obtain a clean bottle. A ketchup bottle will do. Fill the bottle completely with water. Hold your hand tightly over the mouth of the bottle, and then turn the bottle upside down into a dish or bowl of water. Take your hand away when the mouth of the bottle is underwater. Does the water run out of the bottle? What is keeping the water in the bottle?

6   An experiment with air pressure. Do this activity over a bowl or sink. Fill a glass with water. Place over the top of the glass a piece of card — an index card is ideal.

Hold the card in place and slowly turn the glass upside down. Carefully take your hand away. What happens? Does the water run out? If it does, try again.

If the water stays in the glass, this is because the air pressure is pushing against the card to keep the water in.

Turn the glass around so that the mouth of the glass points in all directions. Does the water stay in the glass? What does it show us about air pressure?

7   Make a coin stick. Breathe on one side of a dime. Press it firmly in the middle of your forehead. The coin stays in place. Why is this? Why is it necessary to breathe on the coin?

8   An experiment with a sink plunger. Borrow a sink plunger.

Slightly moisten the edge of the cup. Then push the cup down firmly onto a smooth surface. A tabletop is ideal; so is a floor that is covered with tiles. Now try to lift the cup away.

Why is it so difficult to pull the cup away from the smooth surface? What is holding the cup to the smooth surface?

When you have released the cup, place it gently on the same smooth surface. Do not press it down at all. How difficult is it to pull the cup away now?

9   Make a siphon. You need a piece of rubber tubing. Start by putting a bowl of water on the table. Hold the tube underwater in the bowl until all the air has bubbled out. Then pinch one end of the tube tightly and bring it over the side of the bowl into an empty jam jar held below the level of the bowl. Let go of the end of the tube and water should flow out.

What happens when you raise the end of the tube in the jam jar? Does water still come out? What happens if you let air into the tube? Where must you place the two containers for the water to flow out the fastest?

The siphon works because of air pressing down on the water in the bowl and forcing it up the tube. Can you think of ways in which you could use the siphon to help you in the home, garage or garden?

10   Make a weather vane. Ask a grown-up to push a knitting needle through a cork for you.

Cut two arrows out of poster board. Make them both exactly the same size. Color the arrows. Obtain an old pen top. Glue one side of each of the two arrows. Stick them together around the pen top. Make sure that the pen is in the center of the arrows.

Stick four toothpicks into your cork. Cut out the four points of the compass (N, S, E, W) out of poster board. Stick them onto the toothpicks, as shown in the picture.

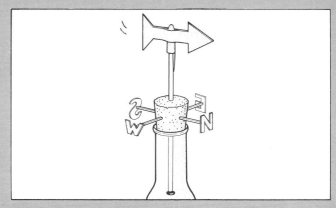

Now rest the cork on top of a narrow-necked bottle and balance the weather vane on top of the needle.

Take the weather vane outside. Ask a grown-up which way is north, and point the N on your weather vane in that direction.

The arrow on your weather vane will be turned by the wind. It will show from which direction the wind is blowing.

Keep a record of the direction of the wind each day for at least a month. Write down whether the wind is strong or gentle each time. From which direction does the wind blow most often? From which direction does the wind blow least often?

11   Observing the wind. Write down six things that you can see happening when a strong wind is blowing.

12   Collect pictures of sailing ships, yachts and windmills. Write a story or a poem about your favorite picture.

13   Collect pictures of the damage done by gales and other strong winds. Make a wall chart with your pictures.

14   An experiment with a balloon. Put an empty balloon inside a plastic beaker. Blow the balloon up while it is still inside the beaker. Squeeze the neck of the balloon so that the air cannot come out. Slowly lift the balloon. What happens to the beaker? Why?

Let the air out of the balloon very gradually. What happens to the beaker now? Why?

15   Lift a 2-pound weight with a balloon. Place a 2-pound weight on the table. Try to move it by blowing it along. Are you able to move it?

Now place a balloon on the edge of the table. Put the 2-pound weight on top of it. Blow up the balloon. What happens to the weight? Why?

16   What happens to the air over a hot radiator? Obtain a short stick. Cut up some paper tissues into long strips about 1/2 inch wide. Glue or tie several of the strips onto the end of the stick.

Hold the strips of tissue just above a hot radiator. What do you notice? Why is that?

17   Make a simple barometer. You need a bottle, a dish and two thin pieces of wood. A tall bottle or a jar made from clear glass is ideal.

Fill the bottle with water. Hold the dish over the top of the bottle, and turn the bottle upside down quickly but carefully. Some of the water will spill, so do this part over the sink.

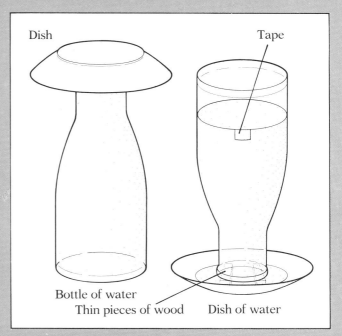

Dish

Tape

Bottle of water

Thin pieces of wood   Dish of water

Put the bottle on a shelf where it can be left. Tilt the bottle slightly to let some more air in. The bottle should be about one-third full of air. Rest the neck of the bottle on the two pieces of wood so that water can move in and out of the bottle. Stick a piece of tape on the bottle and mark the level of the water at the start of your work.

When the air pressure increases, it forces the water in your bottle **up**. When the air pressure falls, the level of water in the bottle will also **fall.**

See how the level of the water in your bottle changes from day to day. Keep records of the weather when the air pressure is low and when it is high. What do you notice?

Fire

Things that burn need air. A sheet of paper burns well because a lot of air can get to it. If the sheet of paper is rolled up into a ball, it burns only at the edges. The air cannot get to the middle of the ball.

When you build a fire you arrange the wood and paper so that plenty of air can get to them. A fireplace has holes in it to let the air in that helps burn the wood. If a fire does not burn well, people sometimes blow it or fan it with a piece of cardboard so that it gets more air. It is the oxygen in the air that is needed for burning.

Sometimes we want to stop fires from burning. To do this we stop air from getting to the fire. Many fires are put out with water. The water cools the fire and stops air getting to it. But water cannot be used against fires where gasoline or oil is burning. These float on water and keep burning. Fire fighters spray oil and gasoline fires with foam. The foam stops air from getting to the fires and puts them out. A good way to save someone whose clothes are on fire is to wrap the person up in a rug or blanket. This stops air from getting to the flames and soon puts them out.

Sheet of paper burning

Ball of paper burning only at the edges

Building a campfire
Using foam to put out a fire on a burning ship

Moving through the air

Seagull rising on a thermal

On a warm day the sun heats up the land. The hot land heats the air above it, and the warm air rises. These warm air currents are called thermals.

Some birds use these air currents to help them to fly. The pilots of gliders and hang gliders also use thermals to carry them higher. Air slows down the things that pass through it. A sheet of paper falls more slowly than a paper ball. The way air slows things down is sometimes very useful.

A parachute being used

What is happening in this picture?

If a pilot has to escape from his aircraft, he uses a parachute. The air catches in the parachute and slows it down. The parachute brings the pilot to the ground slowly so that he or she does not get hurt. If a car or an airplane is to go very fast it must be streamlined. This means that it should be made smooth and slim so that air moves over it easily.

Fast-flying birds such as swallows, swifts and martins are also streamlined so that the air goes past them easily.

Concorde — a streamlined airplane

Flying animals

Many living things can fly by themselves. Birds, bats, and most insects have wings with which they fly through the air. The first flying animals were insects. We know from fossils that there were flying insects on earth millions of years ago.

A fossil dragonfly

Insects that have two wings are called flies. There are more than 85,000 kinds of flies in the world. The housefly and the bluebottle or blowfly are very common. So is the little yellow and black beefly. The beefly looks like a bee but it is really a fly because it has only two wings.

Bees, wasps and dragonflies have four wings. So do butterflies, moths and beetles. Although beetles have four wings, the outer two are not used for flying. They are hard and form a case that protects the delicate pair of wings used for flying.

A bluebottle or blowfly

A dragonfly

A butterfly

Birds

It is not surprising that something as small and light as an insect can fly. But birds are able to fly great distances even though they are quite large.

The largest swan is the trumpeter swan. Trumpeter swans can grow to 5½ feet long with a wingspan of 10 feet. A swan can fly very well. The body of a swan, like that of all birds, is built for flying. Its bones are hollow and light. The swan's body is streamlined. The wings of swans and other birds are a special shape. They are rounded above and hollow underneath. When air moves past the wings they tend to lift the bird upwards. A swan runs along the water when it wants to take off. When the air moves fast enough past its outstretched wings, the swan will rise into the air and fly.

In the air birds push themselves along by flapping their wings. When the wings flap down they push the bird forward through the air. The tail of the bird steers it. The tail and wings also fan out to slow the bird down as it lands.

Swan taking off

Swan's wing

The inside of a bone from a swan's wing

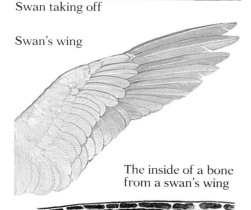

A bird about to land

19

Balloons

The first-ever flight by humans was made in a balloon by two French brothers. The balloon was very light and it had an open neck. The balloon was made of linen. A small fire was lit under the bottom of the balloon. The balloon quickly filled with hot air. Hot air is lighter than cold air. So the balloon soared up into the sky.

Hot-air balloons are still sometimes seen today. Instead of having a fire under it, a gas flame is used to heat the air inside the balloon. Hot-air balloons cannot travel fast because they are carried by the wind. But they can carry only two or three people.

Balloons are also used today to study the weather high in the sky. These balloons are made of thin plastic. The balloons are filled with a gas called helium. Helium is lighter than air and so the balloon rises. Toy balloons do not fly very well. This is because they are filled with compressed air, which is quite heavy.

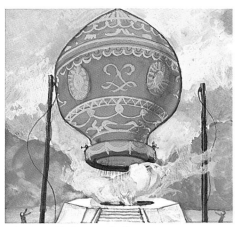
The first flight in a balloon

A modern hot-air balloon

A weather balloon

What do you think this is? What is it filled with?

20

Airplanes

A propellor-driven airplane

A jet airliner

Airplanes are much heavier than air. But they can travel through the air. Some airplanes have propellers turned by powerful engines. The propellers move the air against the airplane's wings. The wings of an airplane are shaped so that air moves faster over them than underneath them. This lifts the airplane upward. When the air is moving fast enough, the airplane takes off and flies.

Many airplanes have jet engines. Air is taken in at the front of a jet engine. The air is squeezed or compressed into a small space by the engine. Then the compressed air is heated. The hot air rushes out of the back of the engine. This pushes the jet airplane forward. Jet engines are very powerful. So a jet airplane moves very fast over the ground before it takes off. As it moves over the ground, air rushes past its wings. The moving air lifts the jet airplane.

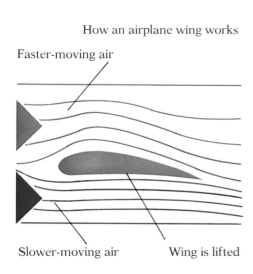
How an airplane wing works
Faster-moving air
Slower-moving air   Wing is lifted

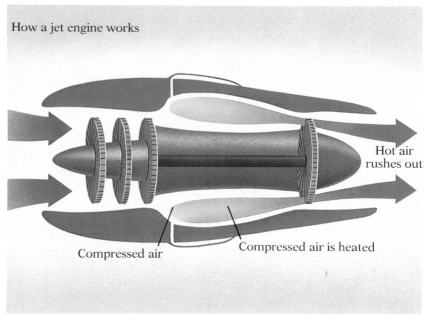
How a jet engine works
Hot air rushes out
Compressed air   Compressed air is heated

21

Keeping warm

A cold wind quickly makes you shiver. Your body is losing heat to the moving air. When you shiver, your muscles are making more heat to warm your body. In cold weather we wear extra clothes. These keep the wind from moving around our bodies and making us cold.

Even houses can lose heat to the air in cold weather. Much of the heat from our furnaces is lost through the windows, walls and roof. Cold moving air, called a draft, also comes into the house through cracks in the door and window frames. We can stop drafts and make our houses warmer by sealing up cracks in the door and window frames. We can also line the inside of the roof and the space in the middle of the walls with a material that keeps heat in.

Some windows are double glazed. They have two sheets of glass with a space in between. The air in the space is still. It does not let the heat escape through the window so easily.

The inside of a roof lined to keep the heat in

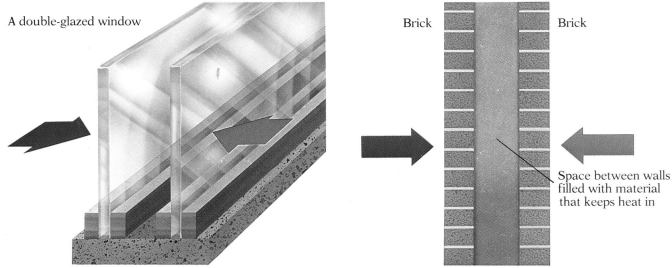

A double-glazed window

Brick

Brick

Space between walls filled with material that keeps heat in

22

Air is one of our most precious things. Without air we would quickly die. In the country the air is clean and pure. City air is much dirtier. We say that the air in cities is polluted.

When anything burns it gives off smoke and fumes. Although we cannot see these fumes they are poisonous. Houses and factories burn coal and oil and produce lots of smoke and poisonous fumes. The engines of cars and trucks make smoke and fumes. In many cities the air is full of dirt and fumes. It gets into our lungs and makes us ill. Now people are trying to make the air in cities cleaner.

Unfortunately there are still many people who smoke cigarettes. These too give off poisonous fumes and pollute the air. Cigarette smoke damages the lungs, making it harder for people to breathe. Cigarettes shorten the life of people who smoke them.

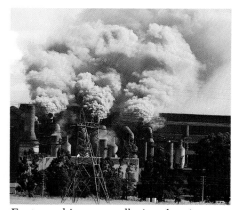

Factory chimneys polluting the air

Fumes from a car engine

A smoker

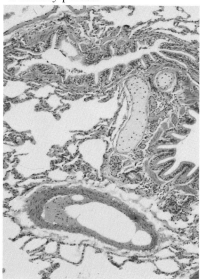

The inside of the lungs of a healthy person

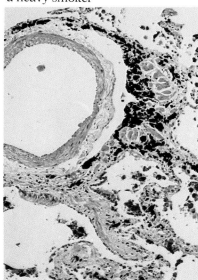

The inside of the lungs of a heavy smoker

Do you remember?

1 What part of the air is needed for burning?

2 What must we do to stop something from burning?

3 What does water do when it is put on a fire?

4 Why cannot water be used to put out oil and gasoline fires?

5 What are thermals and who uses them?

6 What shape must an airplane or car be if it is to go very fast?

7 Name some animals that can fly.

8 What are the outer pair of wings on a beetle used for?

9 What is the largest swan?

10 What shape are a bird's wings?

11 What does the tail of a bird do?

12 Which gas is used to fill the balloons used to study the weather?

13 What does a jet engine do to the air it takes in?

14 How does the air move across an airplane's wings?

15 When you stand still in a breeze, why do you soon feel cold?

16 What happens when we shiver?

17 Where does much of the heat from the furnaces in our homes go to?

18 What word do we use to describe the dirty air in our cities?

19 How does the air in our cities get so dirty?

20 Why is it harmful to smoke cigarettes?

Things to do

1 **Collect pictures that show the different ways in which people have kept themselves warm throughout history.** Make a series of wall charts of your pictures.

2 **Write a poem called "Fire!"** Make some music to go with your poem. What instruments will you use to make the crackling sound of the flames? Write down your music if you can.

3 **An experiment with poster board.** Obtain a large sheet of poster board. Get a partner to help you to hold the sheet upright between you. Run with it across the playground. What do you notice?

Now hold the sheet flat between you and run. What do you notice? What is the difference?

Hold only one corner of the sheet of poster board each. Let the sheet hang down limply. Now run fast with it. What happens?

4   Make a model parachute. Obtain a piece of cloth or thin plastic wrap about the size of a handkerchief. Tie pieces of string, each about 1 foot long, to the four corners of the cloth or plastic. Tie the other ends of the string to a large metal nut or washer.

Fold the whole parachute into a loose ball. Throw it high in the air on the playground, away from buildings and overhead wires. Watch the parachute open. Why does it come down slowly? Try it with weights of different sizes.

Real parachutes have a small hole in the top. Why is this? Cut a small hole in the top of your parachute. What difference does it make when you throw your parachute up and watch it come down again?

5   Make a paper dart. Fold an oblong piece of paper along the dotted line. Fold the corners (aa) into the middle.

Now fold the two new corners (bb) into the middle.
Next fold two new corners (cc) into the middle.
Fold the dart in half upward.
Straighten the wings and fasten them together with tape.

Hold your dart between your thumb and first finger and throw it forward. Does it glide? Why?

Try adding a little piece of clay or a paper clip to the front of the dart. Now throw the dart. Does it fly better? Add more weights to the front and see what happens.

What happens if you bend the tip of the dart to one side? Why does it happen? What happens if you bend the tips of the wings?

Try making darts of different sizes. What is the best size? Try making darts from different kinds of paper. Are the best gliders made from newspaper, drawing paper, glossy magazine paper or construction paper?

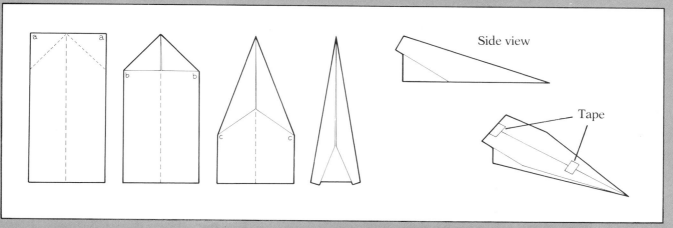

Side view

Tape

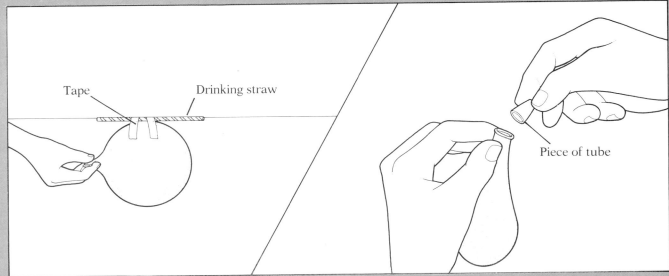

Tape Drinking straw

Piece of tube

6 Make balloon rockets. Blow up a balloon. Squeeze the neck of the balloon so that the air cannot escape. Now let the balloon go. What happens? The air rushing out of the balloon pushes the balloon in the opposite direction. In the same way, the hot gases rushing out of a rocket or jet airplane push the rocket or airplane in the opposite direction.

Obtain a spool of thread. Push one end of the thread through a drinking straw. Tie the thread tightly across the room.

Cut two lengths of clear tape. Blow a little air into the balloon. Attach the balloon to the straw with the tape. Blow some more air into the balloon and squeeze the end to keep the air from coming out. Now let the balloon go. What pushes the balloon along? How far does it travel?

Set up two balloon rockets side by side. Have races with them. See how far they go when one has less air in it than the other.

Do the balloon rockets work better if you fit them with a nozzle? You can make a suitable nozzle by cutting a piece of the tube from an old ballpoint pen. Fit the nozzle to the balloon as shown in the picture.

7 Pretend that you are going to make a journey around the world in a hot-air balloon. Look at an atlas to see which countries you would visit. What seas, mountain ranges and deserts would you cross? Write a story describing some of the adventures you have.

8 Collect pictures of animals that fly. Stick your pictures in a book and write a sentence or two about each one.

9 Find out about airliners. Collect pictures and find out all you can about one kind of airliner. Make a book about the airliner you have chosen.

10 Write a funny story. It should be called "The man who could not stop smoking."

Experiments to try

Do your experiments carefully. Write or draw what you have done and what happens. Say what you have learned. Compare your findings with those of your friends.

1 Can we weigh air?

What you need: Some thread; some drinking straws; two balloons; some paper clips.

What you do: Tie a piece of thread to the center of a drinking straw. Hang the straw from a hook in a part of the room where there are no drafts.

Slide a paper clip onto each end of the straw. Blow up two balloons. Blow them up until they are quite big. Twist the necks around and tie them with thread. Tie one with a bow so that it can be untied quite easily. Now tie one balloon to each end of the straw. Move the two paper clips along until the straw is level.

Then carefully loosen the thread on one balloon — the one tied with a bow — and let the air out. What happens to the straw?

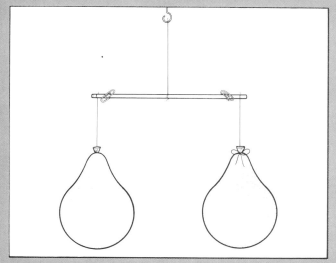

Does the balloon weigh more or less now? Does air have weight?

Hang more paper clips onto the end of the straw where the empty balloon now is. How many paper clips weigh the same as the balloonful of air?

2 How fast do you breathe?

What you need: A watch or a clock with a second hand.

What you do: Ask a friend to help you. Sit down quietly on a chair and ask your friend to see how many times you breathe each minute. It is best to do this three times and to find the average of the three counts.

Find out how many breaths you take in a minute after you have:

a been standing for 5 minutes
b walked quickly around the playground
c run around the playground
d jumped up and down for a few minutes

Show your results in a block graph.

What do you notice about the number of times you breathe each minute after you have carried out these various exercises? When do you breathe the fastest? When do you breathe the slowest?

Now change places with your friend. Does your friend breathe faster or slower than you did after doing the exercises? Is your friend bigger or smaller than you are? Is your friend better or worse at sports than you are?

3 How much air do your lungs hold?

Do this experiment with your teacher.

What you need: A large plastic bottle that holds 1 gallon; a large bowl; a piece of rubber tubing about 2 feet long; a tumbler containing a weak solution of an antiseptic such as a mouthwash; a ruler; some rubber bands.

What you do: Fill the bottle to the top with water. Put some water in the bowl (not too much or it will overflow later). Hold your hand tightly over the top of the bottle of water. Quickly but carefully turn the bottle upside down so that the top is under the water in the bowl. Take your hand off the top of the bottle. The water will not run out of the bottle. Ask someone to hold the bottle still for you. Attach a ruler to the side of the bottle with rubber bands.

Put the tube in the neck of the bottle, as shown in the picture. Take a deep breath.

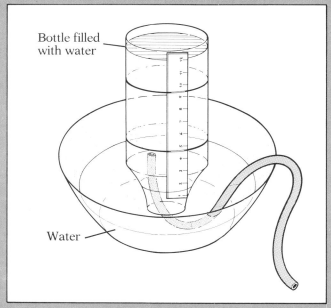

Hold your nose, and blow down the tube. The more air you have in your lungs, the more water you can blow out of the bottle. Measure the distance between the bottom (now the top!) of the bottle and the level of the water.

How much air do your lungs hold?

Instead of taking the biggest breath you can, just take an ordinary one. How much smaller is this ordinary breath than the biggest one?

When do you breathe deeply? Who has the biggest lungs in your class? After each person has blown down the tube, dip the end in a weak solution of antiseptic to kill any germs. Do the biggest people have the biggest lungs? Do the smallest people have the smallest lungs? Are the people with the biggest lungs better at running, swimming or other sports than those with smaller lungs?

4 Burning candles

Do this experiment with your teacher.

What you need: Some short pieces of candle (about 1 inch long); some jars of different sizes; some old saucers.

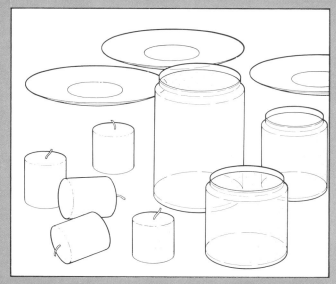

What you do: Carefully run a little water into a saucer. Put a short piece of candle into the middle of the saucer. Light the candle and slowly lower a jam jar upside down over the flame. What happens to the flame? Why?

What happens to the water? Why?

Now do the experiment again using two saucers of water and two pieces of candle. Light both pieces of candle. Slowly lower a large jar over one candle and a small jar over the other.

Which candle goes out first? Why? What happens to the water in each saucer? How do you think the air in the jars is different now from what it was before you lowered the jars over the lighted candles?

5 Experiments with toy sailing boats

What you need: A boat shape made from a small block of wood (balsa wood is ideal, but any piece of soft wood will do); a long nail; some index cards; scissors; drinking straws.

What you do: Hammer a nail into the center of the boat. This will be the boat's mast. Cut a square of card for the sail, as shown in the picture.

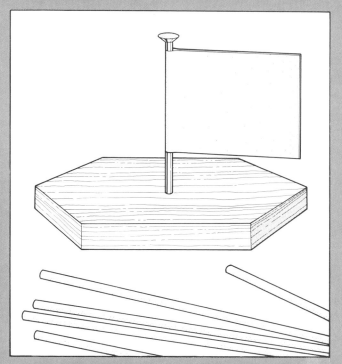

Float the boat on water. Blow through a drinking straw at the sail of the boat. Does the boat move? In which direction does it go? How far does it go? How can you make your boat turn to the left or right?

Now experiment with sails of different shapes and different sizes. Again use the straw to blow into the center of the sail. Measure how far the boat goes with the sails of different shapes and different sizes when you give it one big blow.

Which sail makes the boat go the greatest distance for one big blow?

What is the biggest sail you can have on the boat without its turning over?

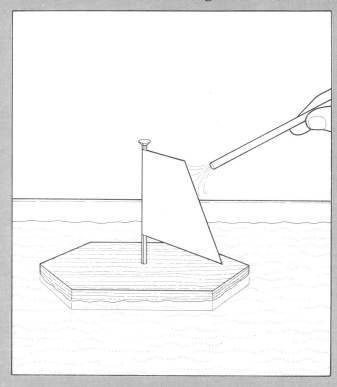

6 Which materials will keep water warm the longest?

Ask your teacher to help you with this experiment.

What you need: Three cans, all of the same size, three thermometers; some squares cut from old clothing — wool, silk, cotton, and so on — and other materials such as cotton batting, feathers and a piece of real or artificial fur; some rubber bands or glue; a clock or watch.

What you do: Arrange your three cans on a level table where they cannot easily be knocked over. Wrap a square of woollen cloth around one can. Put a layer of cotton or silk cloth around the other. Fasten the two pieces of cloth with rubber bands or glue. Leave the third can without any cloth around it.

Heat some water in a kettle until it is hot but not boiling. Then ask your teacher to pour the hot water into all three cans so that they are all filled to the same level.

Place a thermometer in the water in each of the three cans. Write down the temperature of the water in each of the three cans. Every 10 minutes write down the temperatures again. Keep on taking the temperature of the water until the temperature does not fall anymore.

You might draw a table like this:

Time	Temperature Can 1 (no cloth)	Can 2 (woollen material)	Can 3 (cotton material)
11·00	150° F	150° F	150° F
11·10			
11·20			
11·30			
11·40			
11·50			
12·00			

What effect does the material around the cans have? Which material would make the warmest clothes to wear in the winter?

Make a graph of the way in which your three cans lost heat. Does the water in the three cans finish by being the same temperature as the air in the room, a higher temperature or a lower temperature?

Experiment with other kinds of materials around the outside of the cans — furs, feathers and felt are good ones to try. What happens if the cans are put inside cardboard boxes packed with newspaper, sawdust or cotton batting? If you can get the same material in two different colors, for example a light and a dark color, see which of these lets the water lose the heat the quickest.

You could also try the experiment with only two cans — a large and a small one. Do not put any material around either can. Which can loses heat the quickest?

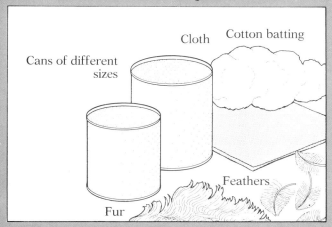

Does this last experiment tell you why human babies and baby birds and animals have to be kept warm in winter?

7 Bottle music

In space it is completely quiet. This is because sounds need air to travel in. In this experiment we are going to see what sounds bottles make when they have different amounts of air in them.

What you need: 6 or 8 bottles, all of the same size (cola bottles will do); a spoon.

What you do: Arrange your bottles in a row. Do not put anything in the first bottle. Put 1 or 2 inches of water in the second bottle. Put a little more water in the third bottle, and so on. Completely fill the last bottle with water.

Use the spoon to hit the bottles. Listen to the sounds they make.

Which bottle makes a high sound? Which bottle makes a low sound? Can you play a tune on your bottles?

How do you know that it is the air and not the water in the bottles that is making the different sounds?

Try blowing across the top of the empty bottle? What happens? Now try blowing over the top of each of the other bottles in turn. What do you hear?

31

Glossary

Here are the meanings of some words that you might have met for the first time in this book.

Atmosphere: the big layer of air that covers the earth.

Barometer: an instrument that is used to measure the air pressure. It helps us to tell what the weather is going to be like.

Carbon dioxide: one of the gases in the air. The air that we and animals breathe out contains more carbon dioxide than the air we breathe in. Plants use carbon dioxide to make their food.

Chlorophyll: the green substance in leaves. It is with the chlorophyll that plants make their food.

Compressed air: air that has been squeezed into a small space.

Draft: cold, moving air that comes into houses through cracks in the doors and window frames.

Fossil: the preserved imprint of a plant or animal found in rock; the preserved hard parts of the plant or animal itself.

Helium: a very light gas that is sometimes used to fill balloons.

Lungs: the two large, spongy bags in our chest on either side of our heart. Inside our lungs some of the oxygen goes from the air we breathe into our blood.

Mineral salts: the chemical substances that plants obtain from the soil and use as food.

Oxygen: the gas in the air that goes into our blood when we breathe in. Oxygen helps our food to give us energy. It is also needed when something burns.

Pollution: the dirtying of air or water.

Streamlined: something that has a smooth, slim shape, so that the air (or water) moves over it easily, is said to be streamlined.

Thermal: a warm air current that travels upward.

Tornado: a very fierce storm that causes great damage to houses and ships.

Vacuum: a completely empty space.

Wind: moving air.

Windpipe: the tube that leads from our mouth to our lungs.

Acknowledgments

The publishers would like to thank the following for permission to reproduce transparencies:

Airship industries p. 20 (left); C Alexander p. 8 (top right), p. 9 (bottom left); Heather Angel p. 6 (left); Ardea: J D Bromhall p. 5 (top left)/Alan Wearing p. 23 (top left); Barnaby's p. 10 (bottom left), p. 16; BBC Central Stills Library (Jack Scott) p. 11 (right); A Beaumont p. 21 (top left); Bruce Coleman p. 5 (right)/John Pearson p. 8 (center right)/Frieder Sauer p. 18/Stephen Dalton p. 18/A J Deane p. 18/D Washington p. 19; Elisabeth Photo Library p. 2/Roy p. 20 (center right), p. 21 (center left); P & P F James p. 17 (right); T Jennings p. 4, p. 6 (center right), p. 11 (left); London Scientific Fotos p. 23 (center bottom and bottom right); Photo Library International p. 3; Picturepoint p. 5 (bottom left), p. 8 (bottom right), p. 10 (top left), p. 22 (top right), p. 23 (center left); M G Poulton p. 7, p. 10 (top right); G A Robinson p. 20 (bottom right); P H Souster p. 22 (center right); G C Telling p. 23 (bottom left); Vision International: Le Cossec p. 9 (top right)/Heini Schneebek p. 9 (top left); ZEFA p. 17 (center left and bottom left).

Index